for every child who dreams of going to school

Going to School in India is a project of SHAKTI for Children, which is dedicated to teaching children to value diversity and to grow into productive, caring citizens of the world (www.shakti.org). SHAKTI for Children is a program of the Global Fund for Children (www.globalfundforchildren.org), a nonprofit organization committed to advancing the education and dignity of young people around the world.

The support of the North American edition of *Going to School in India* has been provided by the Flora Family Foundation, the Virginia Wellington Cabot Foundation, and the Chintu Gudiya Foundation.

Based on *Going to School in India,* published in Penguin Enterprise by Penguin Books India in 2003

Developed by Shakti for Children/Global Fund for Children
1101 Fourteenth Street NW, Suite 910
Washington, DC 20005
(202) 331-9003
www.shakti.org

Published by Charlesbridge
85 Main Street
Watertown, MA 02472
(617) 926-0329
www.charlesbridge.com

Details about the donation of royalties can be obtained by writing to Charlesbridge,
the Global Fund for Children, and the Going to School Fund (www.goingtoschool.com).

Library of Congress Cataloging-in-Publication Data
Heydlauff, Lisa.
  Going to school in India / Lisa Heydlauff ; photographs by Nitin Upadhye.
    p. cm.
  Includes index.
  ISBN 1-57091-666-7 (reinforced for library use)
  1. Education—India—History—Juvenile literature. 2. Schools—India—History—Juvenile literature.
  I. Upadhye, Nitin. II. Title.
  LA1151.H49 2005
  370'.954—dc22   2004012645

Printed in China
(hc) 10 9 8 7 6 5 4 3 2 1

Printed and bound by Jade Productions
Designed by B. M. Kamath

GOING TO SCHOOL IN INDIA

LISA HEYDLAUFF

Design By B.M. KAMATH

Photographs By NITIN UPADHYE

Foreword by Sushmita Sen

SHAKTI for Children

Charlesbridge

Contents

60

66

50

28

Jam
Kas

Punjab

Haryal

Rajasthan

Gujarat

Mo

83

MUMBAI
Maharashtra

40

Karnataka

Kerala

20

950.000 SCHOOLS

29 States

5.000 unofficial

3 million teachers languages

29 languages are taught in Government Schools

1,000,000,000 text books

There are 348 million kids in India (under age 15)

156 million kids go to school

Every 50km languages change

34

Pradesh

Bihar

Sikkim

Arunachal Pradesh

Assam

Nagaland

Meghalaya

Manipur

Jharkhand

Tripura

Mizoram

West Bengal

Chattisgarh

Orissa

26

72

55

76

10

44

88

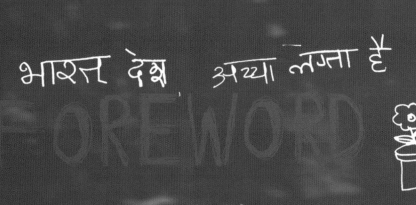

भारत देश अच्छा लगता है

FOREWORD

I have a secret I would love to share. Did you know that going to school is about dreams? Perhaps we should be placing our fingers to our lips and whispering "shhhh," because dreams are often very quiet. Sometimes they live their entire lives inside us without peeking into the light. But there is something I must share with you, something I know: if we believe enough, if we dare, our dreams do come true.

In India we believe in so many things: our families, our religions, our friends, our country, our movies, even what we eat and when. Most of all, we believe in our children. And if there is one place where we can change children's lives, it is by changing the way they go to school. If we make sure there are enough high-quality schools, ramps for children in wheelchairs, paints for all children to color what they dream, inspired teachers who love teaching, activities that explain the world around us, and an environment that lets children be themselves, dreams become possibilities.

Like all children, my five-year-old daughter Renée is a bundle of imagination. Hers is a world of colors, figures, shapes, and sizes, where even the sky is not the limit. It is at school that Renée most often explores her dreams, her

RENÉE SEN

creativity, and her wonder about the world around her. Education is the greatest gift I can give her, and school is the beautiful wrapper it comes in. Every day I cherish the excitement with which she opens this package.

When I read *Going to School in India* to Renée, I can't help but admire the courage, spirit, and hunger for learning of the children in these pages. I salute all the children of the world who dare to dream, and I thank them for keeping the child in me alive.

This book is for all the caterpillars, who will one day be butterflies.

With dreams,

Sushmita Sen
Indian actress, education activist, Miss Universe 1994

Every school day **millions** of children go to school in India in city classrooms, mountain fields, desert tents, and glowing temples. Crossing **great distances**, riding bicycles, wheeling wheelchairs, and waiting for buses on chaotic street corners, they come carrying bright woven bags heavy with books, walking in **flip-flops**, in black buckle shoes, barefoot, and in their uniforms. They come because they **believe going to school can change their lives.** But each day, at the same time, millions of children in India do not go to school.*

All children have the right to go to school and **be inspired.** All children have the right to participate in lessons that can change their lives. All children dream of going to a school that makes learning fun and helps them become who they want to be. And all children know exactly what they would change about going to school— **we just have to ask.**

Going to School in India is a celebration of what school can be.

8

Going to School in India presents many different kinds of schools and organizations, several religions, and diverse children across India—from street kids to kids who go to government and community schools.

Going to School in India, the original concept and book, were made possible by the **Bharti Foundation** in India. The Bharti Foundation believes in helping underprivileged children achieve their **potential through education.**

This edition of **Going to School in India** was made possible by the **Global Fund for Children.** The Global Fund for Children is a nonprofit organization committed to advancing the **education** and **dignity of young people** around the world.

*There are many reasons why millions of children in India do not go to school. Many children have to work to help their families survive or have to stay home to look after their younger brothers and sisters. Some cannot afford the textbooks and pencils they need to go to school. And for others the nearest school is just too far away. Some children find that school is taught in a language they do not understand, or they are treated differently because they practice another religion, or they are too far behind to catch up. Too often schools in India do not have enough facilities for every child. Sometimes there are no ramps for children in wheelchairs, no toilets for girls, or no drinking water or electricity, and teachers are frequently absent. Often facing extraordinary challenges, schools, teachers, organizations, parents, and children are working together to make going to school in India possible for all children and to make school an experience that will change their lives for the better.

9

Getting to school

Getting to school in India can be a wild ride. Every school day millions of children climb into school buses, sit on each other's laps in cycle rickshaws, walk along the edges of mountains, cross scorching deserts on rickety bicycles, and swing across raging blue rivers on dangling swings—just to get to school. Against great odds they come, because they believe going to school can help them realize their dreams. And if it does, it was certainly worth the ride.

Swing

Hundreds of feet above a blue, racing river, Ladakhi children climb into a wooden swing attached to a long cable by two giant pulleys. One of the children reaches up, pulls the rope that moves the swing through the pulleys, and edges the swing out over the drop to send them flying over the raging river below. Arriving at the other side, the children strap on their backpacks and climb two more kilometers uphill to get to school.

18

Rope Bridge

Nagaland is a mountainous state of tangled rain forests. In remote areas, kids must cross blowing bridges such as this one to get to school. Children sometimes place the straps of their schoolbags, woven out of their tribal cloth, on their heads so their hands are free to hold on to the ropes and keep their balance.

Vallam

To cross over waterways in Kerala, children step carefully into vallams—small boats made of solid wood—and are rowed across the still water to school.

17

Chackara

Forbidden in India's cities because they create too much pollution, chackaras (or phatphats) are driven in the rural parts of Gujarat. Made from old Enfield motorbikes that pull brightly painted boxes on wheels, chackaras putt-putt along Gujarat's highways, taking children to and from school.

Horse and Carriage

In India's smaller towns some children get to school by horse and carriage.

Man-Pulled Rickshaw

Only one city in India has man-pulled rickshaws: Kolkata (once known as Calcutta). With flip-flops flopping and bells ringing, men in worn T-shirts and plaid dhotis carefully balance their wooden rickshaws in order to roll the weight of their passengers forward across the cobblestones. This is the oldest kind of rickshaw in the world.

12

Cycle Rickshaw

Cycle rickshaws are all over India. These environmentally friendly vehicles compete with the larger traffic that insists on beeping and polluting. In response, the drivers of the wobbly cycle rickshaws ring their tinkling bells.

Auto Rickshaw

Using natural gas is a way to save India's air. All over the country owners of auto rickshaws have been asked to change to natural gas because it does not eat up the environment; it just dissolves into thin air. Every morning across India children pile into auto rickshaws, hanging their bags on the outside and seeing how many kids can fit inside.

13

Bullock Cart

When the roads are damaged by rain in Maharashtra, giant wooden carts are rolled out and pulled by two hulking bullocks to take children to school.

Bamboo Bridge

Assam gets lots of rain, so land that has been carved into fields often fills with water. Bamboo bridges are built in all directions across the fields so children can get to school by walking across tightropes.

16

Bicycle

Girls rarely ride bicycles in India. But in certain pockets of Assam, girls ride together on their way to class. Knowing how to ride a bicycle gives girls the independence, confidence, and freedom they need to get to school.

15

School Bus

School buses are often painted yellow in India. These buses are helping to save India's air by using natural gas.

Army Truck

Camel Cart

Sometimes kids in the desert of Rajasthan ride camel carts to school.

Patrolling some of the highest sand-blasted highways in the world, the Indian army moves along the line of control between India and Pakistan. High in these mountains there is no official school bus system, but friendly soldiers drive the children to school. They carefully place ladders or wooden planks against the backs of their trucks so that each child, with the helping hand of a soldier, can balance one foot in front of the other and climb inside.

14

If you come across a word you don't know, look for it in the glossary on page 97.

inspiring stories

stories that make you want to go to school

From a tent in the desert to school in the dark, explore 12 exciting stories of going to school in India. And don't forget to take a break for lunch in the middle of your journey.

"Prayer flags are for God, who comes in the wind to blow through them," whispers Tsewang, age 10, as he looks up from coloring a bright line of flags. "God is in the wind," he says, placing a hand on his chest, "and in my heart."

20

Government Primary School Tukla, Tukla Village, Jammu and Kashmir. *Save the Children UK.*

Y IS FOR YAK

Stanzin, age 8, weaves along a footpath on the edge of a mountain in Ladakh. Followed by four boys wearing the same school uniform, Stanzin seems to lead a red stream racing up instead of down. With cheeks shiny red from the cold, they chat in Ladakhi as they climb higher and higher into the sky.

Going to school in a mountain village means you have to be able to climb. Jeeps can go no farther than the roads do, so on foot the boys climb another two kilometers uphill to reach the plateau that holds their government school.

There is no electricity in this school or in the village below, but in the summer months this does not matter—school moves outside where there is plenty of light. Today, high in the mountains where India touches Tibet, 29 kids are learning English in the bright, cold sunlight.

Stanzin

The sky in Ladakh is electric blue, as blue as the ice-cold river, and the rocks are pale white. Ladakh is a high-altitude desert. Ladakhis say this is where the earth meets the sky.

22

"Y is for Yak," Stanzin exclaims, plopping himself down on the red carpet. Stanzin thumbs through a pack of cards with pictures of Ladakhi queens and black yaks. The cards help the kids learn new English words by showing them pictures of familiar things.

Stanzin holds the Yak card in his chapped hands. "Y." Stanzin tastes the letter, listening to the acoustics of 'Y' play in the wind. "Yaks climb," he explains. "My favorite thing in the whole world is my yak, Rokpo. He makes noises like Rrrrrrrrrrrrr," says Stanzin, rolling 'R' from the back of his mouth. "My yak is big, black, and full of thick hair. You need about five of me to make one yak!" And to show exactly what he means, four of Stanzin's friends line up behind him to make a yak. The boys stamp and stomp the dusty ground, but Stanzin stalls the yak's takeoff with a yell: "Wait for the tail!"

Carma, age 3, who comes to school because he wants to, races to catch up. With his arm outstretched, he is the tail.

tail

23

Jigmat, age 10, watches the yak tear around her school in the sky. When the dust settles, she holds up a card showing a beautifully decorated Ladakhi window. "Window," she says, carefully listening to the foreign sounds. Then, holding up a drawing she has made, she swiftly explains in Ladakhi: "I live in a glass room that keeps me warm; it lets the heat in. From my room I can see my vegetable garden. I like looking out of my window because at night I can see the stars." Jigmat looks down at her dusty red uniform, and then out into the wind. "Sometimes I'm afraid and sometimes I feel free."

As Jigmat speaks, Stanzin's yak comes racing back. Crayons are passed from hand to hand, and yaks begin prancing across the children's pages. "I can see yaks, too, from my window," Jigmat says, smiling.

Jigmat

glass house

Jigmat chosket
class yROllno ②
Tukla 10

hos

24

Ladakh gets over 300 days of sunshine a year. Because it is so high up, you can get sunburned even in the winter.

Tundup

"My school is made of stone, wood, and mud. We have one classroom, one storeroom with two steel boxes of books and games, a ball, a ring game, and some skipping ropes. In the winter we keep warm with a firewood stove, but it is still cold. I go home for lunch because I live really close and there is no drinking water at school." Tundup, age 10

25

HAIDER ON WHEELS

Haider, age 10, gets to school in his wheelchair. Every morning Haider's friends arrive at his house half an hour before school begins. They decide who gets to push Haider, tip his wheelchair back, and off they go.

Haider smiles up at his friends as he describes his "wheelie" trails. "The road to school is not a good road: It has mud and gets flooded in the monsoon rains and there are lots of holes." Haider lives one kilometer from Raspunja Free Primary School. This was a long way when he did not have wheels—so long that he did not go to school at all. Now he rolls wherever his friends take him, and they take him everywhere.

At first Haider's mother was worried about sending him to school. She had many questions: How will he go to the toilet? Will he tell his friends he needs to go? Will he be embarrassed? She said no to the friends who brought Haider a wheelchair and no to the boys who offered to take him to school.

But staff from a local nongovernmental organization (NGO) did not give up. Instead they talked to everyone who could help. They talked to the teachers and the kids. They asked everyone to invite Haider to be a part of what was going on, and his friends and classmates did just that.

26

Raspunja Free Primary School, Raspunja Village, West Bengal. *Sanchar*

Ninety-eight percent of disabled children in India do not go to school. The government of India passed legislation that states that every child with a disability must have access to free education. But only when communities, families, and friends help disabled children will children like Haider be *able* to go to school. Disabled children, just like their able-bodied friends, need a friendly environment to achieve their full potential—schools with ramps for wheelchairs, and teachers, parents, and friends who understand what disabled children can do and work with them so their dreams come true.

Haider

Haider's friend Saifur rests his hands on top of the blue backpack that supports Haider's back like a cushion. Saifur explains their schedule. "Haider goes to school every day except when it's raining because he cannot hold an umbrella and we have a hard time pushing the wheelchair through the mud. When it really rains a lot, then none of us go to school.

"In the holidays, Haider gets upset because he misses school. We have a Snakes and Ladders game, so we go to his house and play that."

Haider dreams about what he will do when he is older. Grinning at his friends, he says, "When I grow up, I want to play football."*

Haider began to dream only after he started coming to school—all Haider needed to dream were great friends and some wheels.

27

*Football is the game known in the United States as soccer.

"Shesh Naag, a snake who holds the world on his back, made the earthquake take place on a holiday so that children would not be hurt. He knew that on that day children would not be in school; rather, they would be outside in the fields marching in parades and singing songs. He chose that day so children would not die. But many children did die when they ran home to see if their parents were safe. If we sin more, if people of different religions keep hurting each other, and if we keep treating animals badly and eating them, the earthquake will come again."
Mahindra, age 12

BUILDING MY HOUSE

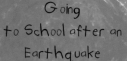

Sitting next to a giant pile of rubble that used to be a government school, 32 young architects are designing the houses they would like to live in. Building their dreams out of the shadows, these architects are creating bright houses of mud, glass, and straw. Glued and pasted together with dusty hands, houses with green doors, holes for windows, flat roofs, and spiraling stairs emerge out of the rubble. As an architect, you have to be very careful when building a house on stones that have shifted because you never know when they might move again.

29

Biku Bhai's House, Bhuj, Gujarat. *Pratham.*

Joyful celebrations on a recent national holiday were interrupted by an earthquake measuring 7.5 on the Richter scale. The earthquake shook Gujarat, destroying countless houses and schools and burying thousands of people under stone.

Biku Bhai owns the house next door to where the children once went to school. For several weeks after the earthquake, he watched the pile of rubble that was their school, wondering. Weeks turned into months, and his thinking turned into an idea. Rather than have the children miss more school, would they like to have school in his courtyard? The teachers agreed and school was opened. The children came, glad to be back together and away from their damaged homes. They would rather sit in the scorching heat in a place with no ceiling than spend more time not going to school.

The earthquake came so suddenly, and destroyed so many lives, that many children wondered why it happened. When there were no answers that seemed right, they found their own. Vanit, age 9, takes a deep breath and explains, "The goddess of the earth, Dharti Mata, felt the earth had become too heavy with sin, so she put it down. That is why the earth moved. But then the god Shankar, who has a third eye and can see everything, told Dharti Mata to pick up the world again. That is why everything is still now."

← Radha's house

30

Now the earth is calm enough for kids to go to school and for their families to build new houses. These kids are constructing houses from their imaginations, houses that will fit into their world and help them come to terms with what they lost. Shilpa, age 8, has not built a house, but she leaps up to visit everyone else's.

Peering into Radha's house, Shilpa exclaims, "It's a Kutchi house!"

Radha, age 9, carefully holds her traditional house at arm's length. It is just like the one she used to have. "No one was hurt when our house fell down, but we lost our TV and we are still digging to find it. We had to sell all of our belongings to be able to build our new tin house."

Shilpa turns and lets her fingers feel their way through the door of Paro's house. Paro, age 7, is wearing a bright dress that matches her blue house. In Paro's house you can play games. "We climb the ladder to get onto the roof and play cricket. There is enough room to bowl, but you might lose the ball over the side. Our house was like this, but it collapsed and now we stay in a hut."

Paro's house

Everyone's house has a story. By building their houses, the children are breathing life into dreams, beginning to believe in possibility, and even imagining houses they have never seen.

Shilpa is almost at the end of her tour. She lies down flat on her stomach, trying to see inside Puja's house. Smiling shyly, Puja, age 8, picks up her brown paper house and places it under her arm. "It needs glue."

Shilpa smiles a wiggly-toothed grin, believing in what glue can do. "My house cracked, too, in the earthquake."

Puja's house

The Gujarat earthquake destroyed an estimated 10,000 schools and 100,000 homes. Creative projects, such as building model houses after theirs have been destroyed, can help children who have experienced trauma express their feelings.

Going to School under a Mango Tree

MANGO TREE PARLIAMENT

34

Extending gnarled, leafy arms as far as it can, a magnificent mango tree casts a giant shadow across the brushed ground. In silence the Ruling Party emerges single file from a path carved into the field. Without so much as a glance at the Opposition, the members of the Ruling Party sit down cross-legged in the shade. The Speaker of the House secures his straw hat and nods in the direction of the note takers, who hold their pencils poised above their lined notebooks in anticipation.

Parliament is in session under a mango tree.

Clearing his throat, the Speaker begins today's session. "Education is the topic of the day." After a long pause, after he has made sure everyone is listening, he continues, "Please proceed." His words hang briefly in the air before the rippling, grassy field swallows them whole.

Scrambling to his feet, Suresh, age 9, a member of the Opposition, begins. "In my opinion, all children in India deserve to get a chance to go to school and to learn things that they would like to learn."

Scratch. Rustle. The note takers begin to scribble.

Suresh scans the crowd, searching for support from his friends. There is no sign of help yet. Shrugging his shoulders, he manages to add in a small voice: "I don't think all children go to school."

35

Community Cottage School, Dubar Village, Uttar Pradesh. *CREDA*.

Standing up, Meera, age 9, the Education Minister, responds, thinking carefully about every word before releasing it onto the Parliament floor. "There are schools everywhere and it is the parents' responsibility to send their children there." Avoiding the Opposition's stares, Meera looks up at the mango tree's stirring leaves.

Suddenly a shout bursts into the wide-open field. "Liar! Liar! You are not telling the truth!"

Meera

"We have seen how Parliament acts on TV, and so we act it out here. It is important to know how to ask questions, to know how to change our lives."
Suresh, age 9

Jumping up and down, the Opposition is on its feet, protesting.

"Liar!" The shouts come in rapid succession.

"Tell the truth or sit down!"

Meera stands her ground. Although she is visibly embarrassed, the Opposition continues to yell. Suresh pumps his fist back and forth to help make his point. "There are villages without schools!" he shouts, full of confidence now that his friends are backing him up.

"Liar! Liar!" the crowd chants, celebrating their own noise. Another boy yells, "When there is one teacher and 300 children, who wants to go to school?"

Suresh

37

Quickly getting to his feet, the Speaker clears his throat. In the momentary lull, he asks in a calm, official voice if the Opposition would mind sitting quietly. Still murmuring, they sit and wait for their next chance to yell.

"I like shouting the most," Suresh confides with naughty delight. "The Ruling Party gives a false statement, and we yell when we know they are wrong. Yelling is the best part; that's why I always choose to be on the Opposition. We yell and the Ruling Party just has to sit there."

Still standing, but wary of the Opposition's ability to explode, Meera begins again. "We appreciate there are not enough teachers and too many students," she says, twiddling her fingers behind her back.

Kamlesh, age 9, a member of the Opposition, demands, "Well then, what will you do about it?" He glances at his friends sitting in the shifting shadows. "You know I didn't used to go to school." Looking back at Meera, he adds, "Nor did you."

Preparing for battle, Meera tightens her red hair ribbon and responds swiftly. "We have opened schools in villages and appointed teachers, but it's up to you, the people, to watch and make it work. We cannot be everywhere." Standing her ground, Meera watches her adversaries warily. The Opposition rumbles, threatening to explode again. But then the President rises. Weighing down the Opposition's bubbling emotions with his open hands, he calmly addresses the Ruling Party. "A point has been made. Take action to make sure there are schools everywhere and that teachers are teaching interesting things." The President sits down on his chair, quite pleased with himself.

The Opposition murmurs, the Speaker clears his throat, and the Ruling Party agrees. Meera, relieved, plops down on the ground. It's official, the Mango Tree Parliament has concluded for the day.

In the scattered light of the setting sun, Seema, age 10, puts her long arm around Meera's shoulder and whispers, "When you know that at any moment the crowd will yell, you really have to believe in what you're saying and have evidence. Otherwise they will just yell and it's all over anyway."

Still a bit rattled from the shouting, Meera smiles silently. Seema hands Meera her backpack and shrugs. "Or else you just have to yell louder than they do." Meera giggles at the thought, and the two girls turn arm in arm to follow several rowdy members of the Opposition home through the fluorescent green field.

Acting out a session of Parliament at their community school gives these children a chance to learn how a parliament works and to practice standing up for what they believe in. Thousands of children in the carpet-making region of Uttar Pradesh do not go to formal government school because they have to work, because they cannot afford uniforms and supplies, and because government schools are often far from their homes. Community schools, built in the children's own villages, give children many of the things they need to attend school: school uniforms, pencils, and lunch.

39

BUS Stop

DOOR STEP SCHOOL

Slowing down in the left lane of a jam-packed city street, a school bus stops in front of a park. Turning off the engine, the driver opens his tiffin tin and spreads his lunch across the dashboard. As he eats, he nods to the kids who jump up the steps and climb past him to take their seats on the floor. When the driver closes his tiffin tin, he opens his newspaper. This bus is not going anywhere, but then it does not need to. Every afternoon, three steps above the smog-filled streets of Mumbai, this stationary bus becomes a school.

"What is a tree?" the teacher asks.

Twenty-three children, name tags safety-pinned to their shirts, peer out of the bus windows at the two trees in the park.

Door Step School, Mumbai, Maharashtra. *Door Step.*

"It's green and brown," answers Joyti, age 11.

"Is that all?" The teacher smiles.

"In the light it is yellow," Joyti continues.

"And red," a little voice peeps out from behind Joyti. Ansal, age 5, tugs at Joyti's dress to show her his creation—a multicolored tree growing out of an orange-edged blackboard.

"I have never climbed a tree, but I would like to," says Lakhan, age 11. "If there were more than two in the park, I would, but I would not want to hurt them."

Lakhan lives near a cinema and repairs plastic buckets to survive, but every day he comes here to go to school. Lakhan loves to read Lot Pot comics. Before he started coming to school, he did not know how to read. Now it is his favorite thing to do.

"Trees grow by eating well and drinking water," Joyti explains, her eyes wide as she realizes just how like a tree she is. Joyti has 10 brothers and sisters, and her whole family lives in this park.

Closing the pages of his comic, Lakhan adds thoughtfully, "We have to worship trees to save them." He pauses, but then continues: "We should make pujas like at the Purnima when women and girls tie red strings around trees, saying prayers and watering them with clean water."

Getting up to find the purple chalk to give his drawing purple plum fruit, Lakhan looks down at the swirling traffic.

"There is no place left to plant new trees in Mumbai," he says, "so we have to look after the ones we have."

42

SCHOOL-ON-WHEELS

Mumbai is a very crowded city with no space to spare. The trouble is that everyone wants to live here. After all, this is where dreams come alive on the big screen. Mumbai is the home of Bollywood, where hundreds of movies are made every year. Once called Bombay, this city has the highest number of residents per square kilometer in India. Apartment buildings climb high into the sky. So when building anything new, including a new school, finding space is the first problem. But a bus can park anywhere, and this one gives the children who live in the park a chance to go to school.

MH·01·H5791

डोअर
स्टेप
स्कूल

Sigma

DRIVE CAREFULLY

43

Parathas are fried chapatis.

chapati and subzi

Jammu and Kashmir
lotus root

India

bhindi (okra)

Chapatis are round,
flat breads made of
wheat, and kids eat
them with subzi
(vegetables) such
as aloo (potatoes),
brinjal (mashed
eggplant), or
bhindhi (okra).

tomater (tomato)

Nagaland
gapha (sticky rice and
cooked meat with spices)

chole (chickpeas)

aloo (potato)

47

Kids from West Bengal pack one treat in their tiffin tins. Usually it is the famous Bengali sweet called rasgulla, which is made from cheese soaked in sugar syrup!

curry

In certain seasons kids in rural Bihar eat boiled sweet potato.

mutter (peas)

Ladakh

Khambir is Tibetan flat bread that is crispy on the outside and slightly gooey on the inside. You can eat anything with it: apricot jam, yak butter, pickle, or even pickled cabbage. Kids walk home for lunch in the wintertime because Ladakhi food does not keep warm in tiffin tins. You need hot soup, thukpa (noodles and vegetables or mountain lamb), and momos (dumplings made of meat or vegetables) to keep warm.

lunch

Lunchtime around India is a multicultural celebration. Rice, daal, chapatis, subzi, sambar, lemon rice, and parathas—kids all around the country eat all kinds of delicious things spiced with chilies, flavored with lime pickle, sweetened with spices, and brought to school in tiffin tins of all shapes and sizes. Tiffin tins are metal tins or lunch boxes designed with multiple compartments. The compartments keep different types of food and sauces from getting mixed together.

mid-day meal

time

day plan

The government of India recently passed a midday meal plan, which means kids in government schools are given lunch at school. That's great news, because for many families the fact that a free lunch is provided is reason enough to send their kids to school.

Where you live determines what kind of lunch you enjoy. It seems everyone eats something just a little bit different everywhere in India.

45

chaval (rice)

chhatu (flattened rice mixed with ground nut seeds and milk)

South India

Dosa is a thin pancake made of rice flour and eaten with coconut chutney.

Lemon rice is made with dry chilies, curry leaves, lemon, and turmeric and seasoned in oil.

gur gur (nat

Puli kuzambu or kara kuzambu (rice cooked in chili or tamarind soup)

Rassam and sambar are thin soups stewed with delicate spices. The soups are mixed with rice, and then kids roll the mixture into balls with their fingers.

In Kerala banana leaves are sometimes used as plates.

Kids bring their drinking water in because sometimes there is no dri

48

Achar is a spicy pickle. Green mangoes are mixed in giant pots with mustard oil and then placed in the hot sun to ferment into pickles.

Tamil Nadu

Today's lunch is greens cooked with coconut, rice, and daal (lentils). Make a ball of rice with your hand and pop it in your mouth. Yum!

moodi (puffed rice) with kheera (cucumber cut into small pieces)

tomato rice

chapati

bean sprouts

al sugar)

Jharkand

tomato chutney, ghobi (cauliflower), boiled rice, and a plantain (similar to a small banana)

ottles and flasks king water at school.

49

GOING TO SCHOOL IN THE DARK

A solitary solar lantern casts blue shadows across the cracked white walls. Devki, the Prime Minister of a Children's Parliament in Rajasthan, sweeps through the room, closing the wooden shutters and sealing the door behind her. It is cold in the desert night.

Devki

Night Schools
In the dusty villages of Rajastha[n] some girls work during the day. While other children go to school, these girls stay home t[o] do housework, care for anim[als] and look after younger brothers and sisters. As the sun sets, they walk to scho[ol] in the fading light. Night schools, taught by teache[rs] from the girls' communit[y] who are elected by the girls themselves, give the[se] girls a chance to go to school after their household work is done[.]

50

Night School, Rampura Village, Rajasthan. SWRC, *Tilonia*

Silently Devki wraps her worn shawl around her shoulders and finds a place to sit. Devki is 13 years old, but she seems much older. She works at home during the day, feeding cows and buffalo and walking several kilometers to collect water from a hand pump. She works at night, too—as a student and as Prime Minister. Devki has a lot of responsibility for a girl who is only 13.

Devki leans forward. "Is there too little light?" she asks the 42 girls sitting in the shadows. The girls nod. It is hard to see, even harder to read. "Electricity is a problem," Devki says as girls bring in two more fluorescent solar lanterns. "Light comes and goes, so we have to make our own from solar batteries. Each night school has a solar tube light, but they are not very strong, so we need lanterns as well. If there are no lanterns, then we go to school in the dark."

During the day solar lanterns store energy from the harsh desert sun. At night they light the night schools with a fluorescent, ghostly light.

Children's Parliament
In Rajasthan a Children's Parliament was created so every girl who goes to school at night would have a chance to learn how a parliament works. Every other year 3,000 girls vote to elect the members of Parliament. Devki and her Cabinet of Ministers have to ensure that the 150 night schools across the district are running well. They go once or twice a month to visit different schools, as Devki is doing tonight. Parliament meets every month, and the members share their reports with the adults who can act on their requests and concerns. Children's Parliaments can be found in other parts of India, too. But Devki's parliament is much more than an interesting exercise. It actually governs how the schools are run.

51

Devki watches the girls fold newspapers in all directions. "It is our school, so we decide what we want to learn," she says, explaining why hats of all shapes and sizes are emerging from the darkness. Devki folds a hat as she tells how she came to be Prime Minister. "I knew I wanted to do something for children, so I thought the Parliament was the best way. I went to each night school and told the girls, 'If you do not have enough paper or if you need new carpets to sit on, I will mention it in the meetings and make sure you get it.'" Devki's eyes glisten as she explains with a half smile, both pleased and shy, "The girls chose me."

Devki is tired from her long day, but to make her dream of opening more night schools come true she needs to ask more questions. "Who lives next to someone who does not go to school?" Hands go up, hats rustle. "If you know someone who does not go to school, can you bring them with you next time?" Everyone nods, but a few girls turn around to watch the door that has just opened.

Santosh, age 13, a Minister in Devki's Cabinet, is standing shyly next to a smiling man. Devki nods and starts to ask another question, but the girls are no longer listening. They watch the man disappear behind a blackboard. Suddenly a puppet pops up, whirling his head wildly from side to side. Devki rocks back on her heels, knowing her questions will have to wait for another night. "Yoo hoo, Santosh, how old are you?" the puppet yells.

"Thirteen," she whispers.

"Is that seven and nine?" the puppet asks. Santosh shakes her head. "No."

"Nine and twelve?"

Santosh shakes her head more furiously. "Thirteen," she whispers, "thirteen."

SMACK, the puppet, kisses Santosh, and the room explodes in laughter.

"Now kiss me; I kissed you!" the puppet insists. As Santosh reaches up to return the kiss, Devki disappears into the cold, dark night. She still has another school to visit tonight.

Santosh

53

JACKFRUITS
+GIANT ANTHILLS

Walk on the wild side with the Paniya tribe. Paniyas are wanderers who collect only what they need. Wandering has always been their way of life.

Vidaya Matriculation School, visiting Chembakolly Village, Tamil Nadu. ACCORD.

Giant jackfruits, prickly and yellow-green, hang high in the swaying trees. Swiveling in the wind, the hard-skinned fruits twist as children weave through the reed grass far below. These children belong to a tribe, and although they often explore their world on their own, they always come back to move together, as one.

Going to school in these red hills means going to school outside; after all, tribal children grow up wandering their world. In fact, children from this tribe are so accustomed to wandering that they used to wander right past the local government school. It just stood too still, and the idea of sitting in a classroom was strange to them. Lessons there are taught in Telegu, which is a foreign language when yours is something else. Although the children paused to look inside, they did not choose to stay.

"Paniya children speak Paniya," Geetha explains, agilely sliding down a slope and striding to the front of the tribe. Geetha's hair glistens ochre in the harsh sun. Geetha isn't sure how old she is. None of the Paniyas know their ages. Wanderers don't seem to need birthdays.

"Elephants do not scare me—they are just hungry, that's all," says Ramesh, holding out a piece of dung.

56

elephant dung →

Marigan, a tribal elder, leads today's expedition. Reaching out to take a glistening green unnichedy leaf in his hand, he explains, "If you get injured when hunting, crush this, make a juice, and put it on your wound." Carefully letting the leaf return to its branch, Marigan leans on his walking stick and follows the trail behind a giant red anthill.

Behind the anthill Rajesh grabs a handful of sharp stems, crushes them in his hand, and holds them to his nose. "The sharp grass smells like lemon, see? It's called pull thailum; it's good for coughs and body pain." But Rajesh is more interested in the other kids, who are leaning into bushes trying to reach something. "It costs a lot in the market," he says, continuing to look over his shoulder, "but here it is free!" Rajesh spins around, racing to catch up with his friends.

Reaching high into the bush with a stick, Rajesh joins his friends trying to catch the green beans twirling in the breeze. "Pumullu kai," he says, reciting the local name for the singing bean. "We don't eat the seeds, but . . ." Rajesh's friend Viji puts the bean to his lips and blows as hard as he can— and an echoing whistle sings.

Viji falls to the back of the trail as he lets a blood-red insect walk from one hand to the other. "We have to know these things because if we are sick, we can go to the forest and cure ourselves. I learned this from my father who learned from his father, like that."

Viji

57

Viji watches the insect scurry to the tip of his thumb and fly away. "Math and English we can learn anywhere; this we only learn here." He smiles. His insect has escaped, but he would have let it go anyway because it belongs in the forest. Viji shrugs, looking ahead to see where Geetha is leading the tribe.

Tribal children rarely go to school because they are not used to sitting in one place. They speak a different language, so they are often treated differently when they go to school for the first time. One day, members from a local NGO visited this village and asked the tribal elders, "If you had your own school, would you send your children there?" The elders thought it was a good idea, and soon a community school was opened where children could learn in their own language. But so they would never forget what their tribe has known for thousands of years, lessons in this community school include forest walks so children can learn about plants, animals, and insects from the older members of their tribe.

Walking through the cinnamon-scented bushes, Geetha is easy to see. Dressed in sapphire, she walks tall and straight as a tree. "It's difficult for us to go to school. Parents need us to help at home, to look after the other children." Geetha's attention is caught by yellow flowers winking in the bright sunshine. Reaching out to touch one, she adds wistfully, "Thottavadi. Touch it—it closes when you do." Geetha continues slowly, sharing a thought or two for every step. "I never went to a government school because there you have to sit in one place. There you cannot walk around. There you are not free to move." Half smiling, she places her tongue on the roof of her mouth and makes the clicking sound of the crickets as she disappears into the thicket. "This school is good for me; here I am free." Her voice and a slant of blue light are all that is left behind.

Geetha

CHANGING MY S
THE MIDDLE

Raindrops break the lake's glass surface, swirling the reflection of the mountains into the cold, gray sky. Namaaz (prayers) echo across the water from a white mosque on the lakeshore, and a shikara skims by carrying two girls, heads covered, on their way to school.

The shikari plunges his paddle into the muddy waters and moves his shallow boat slowly through the island's half-submerged trees until it stops, hitting ground. Balancing one foot in front of the other, the girls step onto a wooden plank that keeps them just above the mud.

CHOOL IN OF A LAKE

The girls walk swiftly past their government school and disappear behind a high wall. School is closed today, but then schools in Kashmir often are. Teachers go on strike or simply do not come. The government closes schools when militant attacks shatter towns and villages, and schools are closed on days like today, when religion comes first.

Government Primary School, Moti Muhalla Kalan Village, Jammu and Kashmir. *Save the Children UK.*

61

School might be closed today, but behind the building all of the children who attend this government school sit quietly on damp woven rugs, as if sharing a secret.

On days when school is closed, the children call meetings of their Children's Group for Development (CGD) to discuss what they can do to improve their school. The children take their meetings very seriously. Although they still live in a world where adults make the decisions, they have chosen to try to change their world—and it seems they have been doing quite well.

Shabeer, age 12, president of the CGD, leans forward, his cheeks crimson from the cold. "We had 200 kids in our primary school and only two teachers. So we decided to go to the chief education officer on the mainland to ask for another teacher. At first he was surprised to see us, but after a minute he smiled and said, 'I have never seen children taking up their own issues; you are most welcome.' We sat and talked for one hour."

Shabeer used to be very shy about speaking in front of others, but today he confidently tells the children's story in Urdu, his own language. "But he didn't give us chai or snacks, and that is what is supposed to happen at meetings, isn't it?" Shabeer smiles mischievously.

A lot has changed in the children's lives since their first CGD meeting, Shabeer explains. "Now children are talking to children about paying attention in lessons. We talk about our problems, which we never did before, and we have also started lessons for working children at night."

Shabeer takes a deep breath and rearranges the mat beneath him, keeping himself just above the mud. On this island it is difficult for children simply to go to school. "When something goes wrong, schools are closed, teachers don't come, and children have nothing to do."

Fatima, age 10, adds, "We still need more space for our school. We have one room, and it's big, but that's where all the classes go on. We need separate rooms because it's dark in there."

Shabeer

Afroza

63

Shabeer opens his right hand and counts finger by finger the points of their plan. "There is much more to be done. The primary school needs to be up-graded to a middle school. Right now as soon as you pass out of the primary school, you have to leave the island to go to another school. Many of the girls drop out because their parents don't think it is safe for them to go that far. When it is windy on the lake, boats are dangerous for girls because they do not know how to swim. Boys swim all the time in the summer."

Gulshan, age 12, has not learned how to swim, but she has learned how to suggest changes for her school. She leads the discussion to the subject of quality. "We still have a problem of making a good school: teachers and students do not arrive on time. And when the teacher talks about moral issues, they help in life, but the other classes. . . " Gulshan shrugs. "Well, I am not sure how they help."

Afroza, age 9, rubs the condensation from her glasses with the edge of her black kameez and smiles with her twinkling brown eyes. "If they taught us in a better way. . ."

Gulshan considers Afroza's suggestion and turns to Shabeer to make sure he knows what she means by quality. "If you have two teachers teaching you the same thing—let's say it's nouns—and one teacher tells you what they are while the other uses lots of examples, the second one is the better teacher. That's the one who would make sure children stay in school instead of staying home."

Shabeer looks thoughtful. There are no easy answers. As if reaffirming his feelings, the rain begins to fall again and the children roll up their woven rugs to go home . . . until the next time school is closed and they meet again to discuss how to make their school a place where everyone wants to be.

BREAKING NEWS

It is Thursday afternoon in the winding streets of Old Delhi, and the traffic is in full swing. Wobbly cycle rickshaws battle for space with lumbering green buses. Taxis honk, narrowly avoiding collisions with bewildered roaming cows.

Every Thursday 12 boys ages 8 to 16 make their way through these chaotic, teeming streets to arrive at an empty dance room in Presentation Convent School. Large and small, short and tall, the boys arrive wearing baseball caps, faded puffy jackets, and jeans held up with string. They come from all over Delhi for one reason—they are journalists with stories to file. Together these boys create a newspaper called Wallpaper that they paste on the walls of Delhi for everyone to read. Wallpaper is a street children's newspaper, and all of the reporters are children who live and work on the streets of Delhi. These boys don't attend formal school—the streets are their classroom—but once a week they teach and learn from each other.

BAL MAZDOOR KI AWAZ *

EDITORIAL MEETING

Sonu, age 13, the editor, walks through the door, asking, "Who has brought interviews today?"

"Say hello!" Raju, age 12, calls out, insisting on a greeting. Sonu laughs and flops down on the floor. The meeting has begun.

Wallpaper reporters are used to starting conversations by asking questions; they often do so when they walk up to street children they have never met to interview them. *Wallpaper* reporters must be kind, sensitive, and sincere to get their stories—and they all are, because they know exactly how it feels to live on the streets of Delhi. They live there, too.

Parvez, age 12, raises his hand to give his report. "I interviewed Mehbuk, who lives in the railway station where I live." Looking down at a page torn out of a notebook, Parvez reads aloud in Hindi:

"My name is Mehbuk. I am a ragpicker and I live in Fatehpur Station in Old Delhi. When I go ragpicking the cops stop me and check my stuff. They take any iron or steel item, and then they beat me because they think I have stolen it. The man who I sell to always gives me less than what it is actually worth. Then when I do have money, and go to buy something for myself, he shoos me away, saying I am a thief."

*The Voice of Working Children

Sonu

Dance Room of Presentation Convent School, Chandni Chowk, Delhi. *Butterflies.*

67

Sonu, intrigued, leans forward: This is "news." "Can you find out more? Who are the cops that beat him? Who pays him less? Our job as reporters is to find out as much as we can so we can help change the situation."

Parvez looks at his article, rolls it up, and puts it into his pocket.

"No, we need it! It's good." Sonu laughs, patting him on the back.

Street Children

Many children become street children because they have been mistreated in some way: beaten at home or at school, overworked, or abused. Some children's families are simply too poor to take care of them. When children leave home in search of a better life, they often sneak onto trains going to big cities like Delhi. Once there, they work and live on the streets, finding odd jobs to survive. Some become chai boys who deliver cups of tea, others work cleaning tables and washing dishes in restaurants, and yet others go ragpicking—collecting rubbish that can be sold. But many stay on the railway station platforms where they first arrived, shining shoes and refilling mineral-water bottles from a tap in order to resell them.

Street children can make enough money to survive, but most of them never go to school again. Many live in the overnight waiting rooms at railway stations, where a bed for one night costs 3 rupees. Some NGOs are working to make sure that street children always have a place to go if they need help. Although few street children go to school, they learn in other ways. To survive on the streets, you have to be very tough and very smart—the streets become your school. Writing a newspaper such as *Wallpaper*, with support from a local NGO, gives the kids a chance to express themselves.

Turning bright red, Parvez hands over his crumpled page, and Sonu moves on to his next reporter. "Javed?"

Javed, age 13, is next, but he has not interviewed any children. Sonu raises an eyebrow. "What should happen to you since you failed to bring a report?"

"Why are you asking me?" Javed replies, surprised.

"As this is a democratic setup, you can decide how you will be punished," Sonu declares.

Javed is saved from choosing his punishment by Afroz, age 9, who whispers, "I don't have a report because I lost my pencil."

Sonu changes from witty editor to kind friend and leans in to whisper, "Don't worry, we will find you another one."

With a small knock at the door, a chai boy arrives, one hand flowering with teacups.

"Teatime!" Sonu announces as the boy hands out chai and packets of biscuits. As he dips his biscuit in his steaming chai, Javed considers why they bring out their newspaper. "A minister gets a fever, it is on the front page; a child dies, and no one cares."

Javed looks into his teacup. It is not easy to live on the streets of Delhi. Sometimes it is even harder to talk or write about it. When Javed writes for his newspaper, he is writing about his life. The interviews he collects from other children could be his own. Javed sinks his biscuit even farther into his teacup and continues:

69

"We bring out this newspaper because we want to show adults, even those who shun us and refuse to speak to us, that being poor will not stop us from telling the world our problems." Sonu, age 12

"Children's problems are neglected. We have a lot of children living on the streets. They get beaten up and they are sick all the time—if we don't write about it, no one will know." When Javed is not on a *Wallpaper* assignment, he collects discarded plastic teacups at the Old Delhi railway station. Depending on how many he collects, he can sell them for up to 50 rupees. Javed has been collecting teacups for three years. Returning his cup to the chai boy, Javed says in a very grown-up way: "We all have dreams, but who knows what will really happen?"

The little chai boy shifts uneasily. His sneakers are too big for his feet, and the laces trail behind him on the floor. Sonu follows the little boy's stare, asking him his name and what his dreams are. Shyly burying his face in his hands, the boy stays silent. Sonu declares, "Perhaps he dreams of becoming a journalist on *Wallpaper* just like Javed."

Javed is busy drawing a picture of a chai boy for the next edition of their newspaper. As Javed draws, the chai boy swings a hand full of white teacups, now stained with tea, out the door and into the streets from which he, and all of these boys, came.

Five hundred thousand children live on the streets of India. Twelve of them have a newspaper to say how they feel.

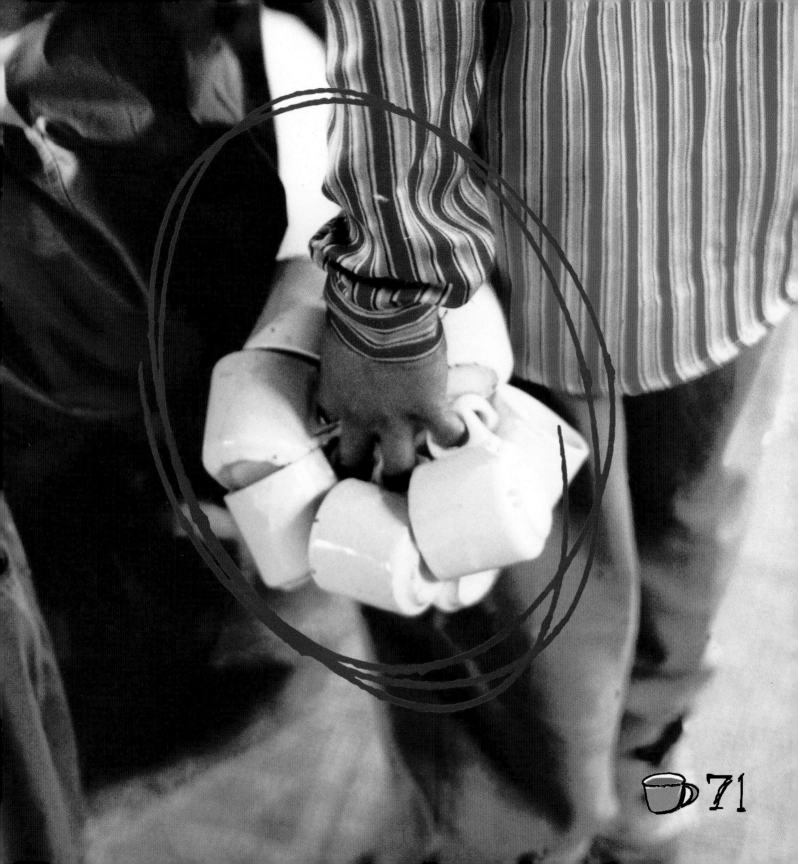

71

PUPPET SHOW

Under a tree on a railway platform, 27 children sit in a semicircle singing about peacocks. It is 8:00 a.m. Trains pull into the station, blowing their whistles, but the children don't seem to notice. A teacher carries a large tin box onto the platform. Catching their breath, the children watch quietly as she awakens the puppets inside. All of these children live and work on and around the railway platform. This is their school.

Two barefoot children jump up, offering to hold the patterned cloth. Ensammee, age 6, dips his hand into the open box and stacks flash cards on the cement floor. Amla, age 9, spins a globe, watching through her tangled hair as the world moves. Another train whistle blows, the children watch the curtain go up, and the puppet show begins.

An orange puppet teacher pops up from behind the cloth. "Wash your hands!" she shouts to a yellow puppet with diarrhea who has not been washing his hands after going to the bathroom.

Acting very sick, the yellow puppet groans loudly. A pink puppet assumes the voice of a doctor. "Drink this each time you have a tummyache," the puppet exclaims. "Just mix water, sugar, and salt, but don't make it saltier than your tears!" Humming happily as she mixes the concoction, the pink puppet spills most of the ingredients, much to the delight of the children. Even the passengers waiting for their train can't help but chuckle.

Train Platform School, Bhubaneswar, Orissa. *Ruchika Social Service Organization and Global Fund for Children.*

Arranging her dusty pink dress carefully around her, Amla sits up on her knees to watch the puppets. "The puppets tell me things I do not know," she says. "That's why I come to school, to see them." Amla searches to see if there might be more left of the show. "I used to collect things all day. I collected plastic bags and sold them to the man who has a shop. Now I bring my rag-collecting bag with me to school so I can start collecting when school is finished. Because I come to school, I get less money, but no one seems to worry because I am learning things."

Amla takes one last look as the puppets go back to sleep in their box. Then, taking her time placing one bare foot exactly in front of the other, she balances along the edge of the platform. "When I grow up, I would like to be a dancer," she whispers, and the small, silver bells on her anklets tinkle as she stoops down to pick up a plastic bag someone else has thrown away.

74

Platform schools give children lunches, baths on Saturdays, books, chalk, slates, and even medical care. Lessons in this platform school focus on things the children need to know to survive and improve their lives. Puppet shows like these help children understand the world around them. The puppets talk about train routes, post offices, police stations, opening bank accounts, the sicknesses you can get from unclean water, who to speak to when help is needed, and the importance of saving money.

Saturday is bath day at the platform school, when everyone comes to school just to take a bath.

FISHING FOR FACTS

நாம் அழைவரும்

Subaramaniye Bharathia Government Girls' High School, Pondicherry on Kuruchukuppam Beach, Pondicherry. *Pondicherry Science Forum.*

IN PONDICHERRY

Hand in hand, a line of girls moves through the cobblestone streets of the old town of Pondicherry. They pass sun-bleached yellow villas, a woman selling pale pink lotus flowers, and a policeman directing them across the road. Some of the girls wear white hats to protect them from the sun. They pass a temple where a painted elephant lives and head to a science class on the beach.

Today these girls are investigating what it is like to be a fisherman. Rather than studying textbooks in their classroom, the girls are going to the source to interview the fishermen themselves.

The girls are divided into five groups. Shanmuga, age 12, is a Fish reporter. Pushing her hat up onto her forehead to better see Kumar, a fisherman, she begins. "What do you do before you go to sea?"

Kumar's skin is tanned black-brown from his days in the sun. Smiling at the girls' official school socks and shoes sinking into the sand, he answers: "I am in the sea for the whole day. There is no before, no after, only sea." Standing barefoot in the scorching sand, Kumar unravels his giant net and lets it fall in fluid layers at his feet.

77

"Where did you learn to fish?" Shanmuga asks Kumar, squinting in the harsh light.

"I learned to fish by fishing with my father, who learned from his father, who learned from his," he answers.

Shanmuga scribbles quickly. "Will your children learn how to fish?"

Kumar eases a fish out of his net. "It depends how much they learn at school, whether or not they get a job; if not, they will come to the sea with me."

Shanmuga scrunches up her nose. "Are you afraid of the moon?" she asks. "People say fishermen are afraid of the moon."

Kumar smiles again. "How can we be afraid of the moon when she brings the waves? We are all children of the sea, and that includes you, too."

Shanmuga closes her notebook and smiles at her new friend.

78

Finished exploring the seashore, the reporters sit down in the sand to share what they have discovered. Malani, age 12, a Plant reporter, begins with a query. "The fishermen say there are blue and yellow flowers under the sea. How can that be? How can flowers grow in saltwater?"

Bala, age 13, a Shell reporter, opens the textbook they brought along for just this purpose. "It can be true! See here, the book has blue flowers that grow in the sea."

Abirami, age 13, a Fisherman's Life reporter, carefully considers what she has found. Glancing up at the fishermen, who have come to listen to her filing her report, she offers, "One fisherman said to me: 'It's good that you come here for projects. Now you know how we live, so when you become leaders, you won't allow foreign ships to come take all the fish.'" Abirami pauses, thinking about what this means in her life. "He made me think that local fishermen need to be given a chance. But how do you do that? I know that I have come to the seaside so many times with my parents, but I did not know this. When we come here to study, we see more. We see how hard their lives are."

Kumanuvalli, age 13, an Imagination reporter, shares her report. "I imagined fishermen must sing songs when they are afraid. Fishermen have an amazing collection of local songs, but when we asked them to tell us, they just shrugged. Most of them cannot read or write, but we know they tell poems about life on the sea to each other." Kumanuvalli watches her friends empty their shoes of sand and unbuckles her own shoes. "Perhaps they did not tell me because I am not a fisherman. One man said, 'We go to all kinds of temples. We are Hindu, we are Muslim, but it does not matter because we are all fishermen.' I am not a fisherman, so perhaps their songs are their secret."

Kalaishanthi, age 12, puts her hands on her friend's shoulders. "It should not matter what religion anyone is because we all have to save the sea. People live along each part of the sea. Our part of the water is the Bay of Bengal. That is why we have to save the sea here. It's ours."

Kumanuvalli nods, sets her purple Imagination notebook down, and takes off her shoes. She grabs Kalaishanthi's hand to pull her into the sea. Tumbling in the waves, the girls squeal as they soak their school uniforms.

"Why is the sea salty?"
Bhanupriya, age 13

81

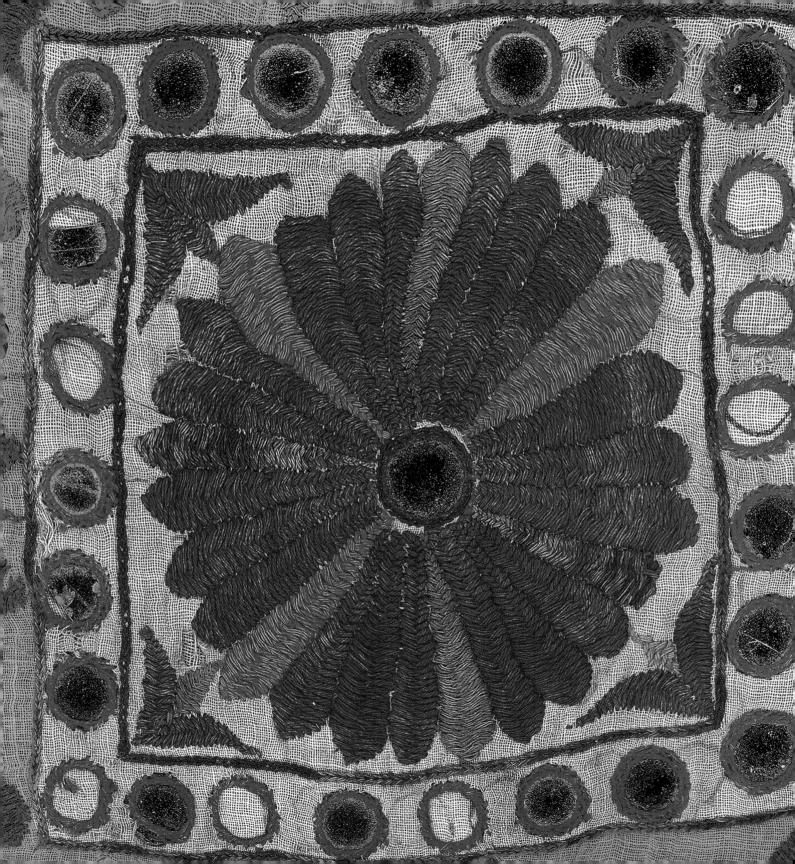

A small, white tent sits on the horizon. The playful wind twists the tent's red flag, and the endless cracked-mud desert melts as mirages hover under the electric blue sky.

गुजरात

GOING TO SCHOOL IN A MIRAGE

83

Ujas Tent School, Little Rann of Kutch, Gujarat. *Ganatar.*

Anji, age 9, walks barefoot through the desert, her green lehenga swaying as she moves. Arriving at the tent, she lifts the flap and disappears inside. Smudged with dust, her tangled hair twisted and woven into tiny braids, Anji sits down and traces the contours of the word *Welcome* that is carved into the smooth mud floor. She is as silent as the desert.

"Anji is deaf and cannot talk. But nobody teases her here," her brother Munna, age 11, explains.

"She likes coming to school. She plays and writes down everything on the board—she gets very upset if I leave her at home."

Anji

Munna follows Anji's stare as she looks up above her. Munna sees what Anji sees: a ceiling fluttering with lime green, pink, and blue paper flags and orange tissue-paper lanterns. Munna sees their school: a tent, glowing like a lightbulb in the desert light. In this mud desert in the Little Rann of Kutch, there are no trees, no animals, and no birds. But there are children going to school. The water beneath the ground is salty, so drinking water has to be delivered by chackaras.* Chackara drivers deliver water for free to the tent schools because the drivers know how important it is for children to go to school.

Every year, the June monsoon rains turn this desert of 12,000 square kilometers into a sea. Water levels rise as high as one and a half meters (taller than any of the children in this tent school). When the rain ends, the water seeps slowly into the ground. From November until May, salt-pan workers and their families move 25 kilometers or further into the mud desert to collect salt. They build makeshift houses, spread across the desert, and install pumps to bring salty water from under the ground into surface basins. The water crystallizes into millions of tiny six-sided salt cubes. Children move into the desert with their families, and tent schools are pitched in the center of the far-flung circles of salt-pan workers' houses. Many children would stop going to school if it were not for a tent school nearby. The tent schools and the government schools work together to keep track of children's attendance and to make sure the children don't miss a beat when they return to their government schools.

*See the "Getting to School" foldout that starts on page 10.

Munna

85

Kneeling beside a tray of precious freshwater, the children take turns blowing drops of oil paint into delicate designs. Anji dips in a piece of paper, admires her creation, and carefully carries it out into the desert to dry.

Just as there is no water in this desert, there is no electricity. Raju, age 10, explains, "We had TV in the village, but here we have not seen it for a while. I don't like it when we have a holiday from this school in the desert because then I do not get to see my friends or watch TV. I always wait for Monday to go to school."

Munna marches past, carrying his oil painting outside. "If we stay at home we have to work, watch the noisy pump, and make sure nothing breaks. You can get hurt. It is much better to come to school. We come when we see the mirror."

Tent-school teachers call children to school by catching light with a mirror and focusing that light on a distant house. Sounds of voices or school bells are lost in the desert. When the kids see the reflecting light, they know it is time to come to school.

Chunda, age 10, raises his voice because he has some suggestions. "We have a mirror, but we need another mirror to see how we look and make our hair nice, a drum to sing songs, a cricket bat and ball, and, because we have used them all up today, more paints." Standing up, Chunda continues, "And more bicycles so everyone can come to school! I come here because I want to be a teacher in the tent school so I can do something good for salt-pan workers." Chunda walks toward the door and dips out of the tent, announcing, "Lunchtime!"

Seeing the other children collect their tiffin tins, Anji does the same. She finds a place to sit in the shade and opens up her tiffin tin to share her lunch with her friends. Tearing a piece of chapati, she rolls the soft flat bread in her sun-baked hands and watches the wind play with the edges of her oil painting in the desert.

Ramesh, age 6, his sister, Samta, age 12, and his brother, Chunda, age 10, ride three on a bicycle to school. They travel six kilometers, and it takes them one hour. Ramesh has a red bandage around his ankle because his foot got caught in the bicycle wheel.

87

WHEN I GROW UP

Children across India have bold, colorful dreams of who they will be when they grow up. What it takes are schools that make learning fun, where children can thrive and realize their dreams.

Paper flowers

"When I grow up, I will make paper flowers. I will wear them in my hair and make garlands around my neck." Reshma, age 9, Madrasa Masaudhi, Malkana Village, Bihar

भारत INDIA

Computer teacher

"E-mails travel by magic." Amina, age 14, Mahita Computer Center, Ganga Dowli, Andhra Pradesh

"I would like to have a mango orchard." Subrat, age 8, Sri Aurobindo Purnanga Vidya Pitha, Karanji, Orissa

Policeman

"Every day I used to go to the docks and steal fish when the boats came in. When I grow up, I want to be a policeman and catch people like me." Manoj, age 11, Ganesh Murti Nagar, Mumbai, Maharashtra

mango

I want to be a

"I want to be a dancer." Tumpa, age 9, Jabala, Kolkata, West Bengal

dancer

I want to be a

Hafiz

"I want to be a hafiz." Saidur, age 8, Islamia Muktab, Thicksay, Jammu and Kashmir

"I think I would like praying all day and being on the top of the mountain." Jigmat, age 6, Government Primary School Tukla, Tukla Village, Jammu and Kashmir

monk

I want to be a Philosopher

"I will travel to teach Buddhism... do good things and think good things. Don't lie, don't create conflict, don't harm anybody. And if people ask what we can really do, I will tell them to look at the person next to them and just ask them how they are." Lobzang, age 12, Chora School, Likeer Gompa Monastery, Jammu and Kashmir

I want to be

I want to be a teacher

"I'd hang paper cuttings from the ceiling and make more windows so the paper can blow, and then I'd play music." Reshma, age 9, ALP Government School Nochupully, Mundur, Kerala

"gypsy"

"I will ride on a camel." Sukhi, age 8, Shepherd's development project, Virami Village, Rajasthan

"I will drive people back and forth from my village to Kohima. I'll charge five rupees—it's the right amount. If you bring chickens I won't charge you extra." Radi, age 9, Government Primary School Rusoma, Rusoma Village Nagaland

भारत
INDIA

I want to be a Bus Driver

"I will be a scientist in Bombay. I want to create medicines so cancer patients and AIDS patients can survive, and I'll discover how to make diamonds, too." Ayesha, age 11 Loreto Sealdah, Kolkata, West Bengal

Scientist

I want to be a Builder

"My father puts shoes on horses and buffalo, but I don't want to do that. I want to make two-story buildings with slanted roofs." Shajad, age 7, Madrasa Masaudhi, Malkana Village, Bihar

"I want to be a leader to serve the people of India. There have been many great leaders in India." Sanyashi, age 10, Gram Vikas High School, Konkia, Orissa

leader

भारत
INDIA

"I want to be a saint because I don't like a world where people fight and argue. People are losing faith. I know being a saint will not solve the problem, but it will be doing something else: It will be not doing what everyone else is doing." Upendra, age 12, Gram Vikas High School, Konkia, Orissa

I want to be a

saint

"I think that being an ambassador is the best job because then everyone knows who you are, plus my brother lives in America." Surabhi, age 12, Government High School, Patna, Bihar

Ambassador

I want to be a

"Once I went on a train and I saw the conductor—he was wearing long trousers, a pressed shirt, and a jacket with shiny buttons. I'd like to wear that uniform." Lochan, age 9

"I will help people to get down from the high steps." Vimal, age 9

"I'd like to see the different places where the land is yellow." Rup, age 9
Government Primary School, Tengabari Village, Assam

train men

I want to be a Girl

"When I grow up, I still want to be a girl, and go to school and play." Amrita, age 8, ALP Government School Nochupully, Mundur, Kerala

I want to be an archaeologist

"I will be an archaeologist in Israel. People say Jesus is not real, but I would like to find things to prove he is real. I will look at the ruins and see what can be found. I will take a camera and a small tape recorder, so whatever I discover I can record on my tape." Tina, age 11, Loreto Sealdah, Kolkata, West Bengal

I want to be a Writer

"I will teach my mother how to write her name." Fatima, age 9, Bikna Community Cottage School, Dubar Village, Uttar Pradesh

I want to be Amitabh Bachchan movie star

"He is my hero." Sonu, age 9, Pratham school under a tree, Dhabalpura, Bihar

I want to be a District magistrate

"When I am district magistrate, I will make sure all children in this district go to school." Rita, age 9, Bikna Community Cottage School, Dubar Village, Uttar Pradesh

forest ranger

"I will swing in the banyan tree's hanging roots where the air is cool and there is a magical breeze." Kumari, age 10, Sri Aurobindo Purnanga Vidya Pitha, Karanji, Orrisa

भारत
INDIA

I want to swing

"I will wear a khaki uniform and I will guard the jungle ... the trees must be saved."

Kailash, age 10, Shiksha Protsahan Kendra, Bhiriyadol Village, Madhya Pradesh

"My friends and I would go to space and see Jupiter, the sun, planets, and stars. Robots also live in space with satellites. Shiva lives in space, too. I want to fly there and when I see him, I would say, 'Oh, my god!' and then I would ask him how he made all of the animals. Because that was a really great thing he did." Vikaa, age 9, Platinum Jubilee High School, Warangel, Andhra Pradesh

space explorer

93

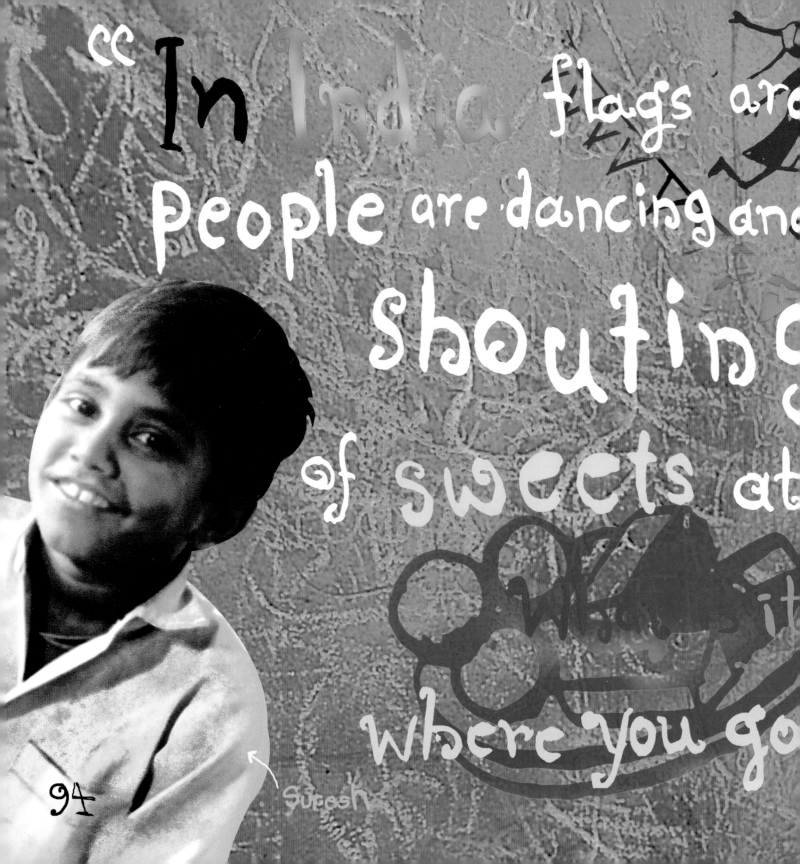

"In India flags are

people are dancing and

shouting

of sweets at

where you go

94

Suresh

always waving singing, doing pujas, slogans, and eating lots festivals. like to school?"

Suresh, age 9, Government Primary School, Bhera Pura Village,
Madhya Pradesh

95

Thank You

You hold in your hands a dream that has been made real by extraordinary individuals who believed in what they could not see—a celebration of what school can be.

Thank you, Justine, for opening the window, Alana for enduring emotions, Kamath for making our project breathe, and Nitin for capturing the light. Thank you so very much to the Bharti Foundation, Sunil, G.K, Hemant, and Tina for believing in possibility and making it come true.

Thank you, Maya and the Global Fund for Children, for recognizing a story within a story, for enabling this book to be read by children around the world. Thank you, Kelly, for your careful steps through words and emotions. Thank you, Cynthia, for communicating with compassion.

Thank you, Radhika, for strategies without horizons, Siddhartha for whimsical suggestions, and Kavita for flair; Hemant and Gautam, trusted trustees; Sanjay for why not, Rahul for details, Chander for fine print, and Cyrus for space to see how far we had come; and to Uncle Don for Isadora.

Thank you, KK, for waving wands; BGVS, Subhash for laughing; Deen, Iqbal, Sharif, and Feroz, Save the Children, UK; Augustine, UNICEF Patna; David, UNICEF Delhi; Ayie, Education Department, Government of Nagaland; Anita and Vinod, Anshumala, BGVS; the Wangnoos, Gurkha Houseboats; Madhav, Rukmini, Sanjib, and B. K. Das, Pratham; Shukdev-bhai and Sheetal, Ganatar; Radha, Mohua, and Sonali, CRY; Biraj, Action Aid; Chappal and Mahesh, Mobility India; Yogendra, Bodh; Satyanarayen, VVKS; Inderjit Khurana, RSSO; Dayaram, EDCIL; Yash from NIEPA, who unfortunately will not be able to see how he helped us to fly, and to all those who we met along the way, thank you for good directions.

Going to School in India stories were chosen because they are inspirational and reflect particular aspects of school in India. We visited many schools across India, but unfortunately we were not able to include a story for each stop on our journey. Our selection by no means passes judgment on the schools, stories, activities, kids, and organizations we could not include. This is a 98-page book. To tell a complete story of going to school in India would require at least 300 million pages, one for every child. But that book, like India's greatest possibilities, really would be endless.

Glossary

Banyan tree: An Indian fig tree with roots that hang down from the branches

Chai: Tea boiled with milk, sugar, and spices such as ginger and cardamom

Chutney: A flavorful relish or pickle, sometimes sweet and sometimes spicy

Cricket: India's most popular game, played outside with a bat, a ball, wickets, and two teams of 11 players each

Dhoti: A piece of cotton cloth worn by men that is tied at the waist and through the legs

Hafiz: A Muslim religious teacher

Kameez: Short for salwar kameez, a long dress with slits on the side, which is worn over trousers by women and girls

Kilometer: A metric unit of length equal to 1,000 meters or 0.62 mile

Kutchi: Characteristic of the Kutch district of Gujarat

Lehenga: A full, flowing skirt gathered at the waist

Line of control: The boundary that divides India and Pakistan in the contested territory of Kashmir

Meter: The basic metric unit of length, equal to 3.28 feet

Mirage: An optical illusion of something that is not really there, such as water in the desert. Mirages often appear over hot, flat, wide-open spaces

Monsoon rains: Heavy rains brought to India in the summer by the southwest wind

Mosque: A building used for public worship in the Muslim religion

Namaaz: Ritual prayer practiced five times a day in the Muslim religion

NGO: Nongovernmental organization (also see below)

Prayer flags: Colored flags with prayers written on them strung by Tibetan Buddhists across their houses, from temples, and in the mountains

Pujas: Prayers offered to Hindu gods

(Vata) Purnima: A Hindu festival during which women welcome the full moon and tie colored threads around a tree trunk and pray for protection for their families

Rann: An extremely dry place

Richter scale: A scale of 1 to 10 used to express the energy released by an earthquake

Rupees: India's currency (45 rupees = approximately 1 U.S. dollar; 79 rupees = approximately 1 U.K. pound)

Shikara: A flat boat used in Kashmir, guided by a shikari

Shiva: A Hindu god

Tamarind: A spice made from the fruit of the tamarind tree

Tiffin tin: A metal tin or lunch box designed with multiple compartments for carrying different types of food

Government Schools, Community Schools, and NGOs

The government of India supports hundreds of thousands of government schools across the country. The government provides buildings, teachers, textbooks, and midday meals. But not all children attend government schools. Instead, some children attend one of the country's many community schools. Community schools are often located in remote areas. Most attempt to meet local needs by offering flexible schedules, teaching in local dialects, and addressing life skills as well as academics.

Many community schools are supported or operated by the hundreds of thousands of nongovernmental organizations (NGOs) across India that work to improve people's lives in terms of education, social welfare, healthcare, and human rights. NGOs work in communities to help ensure that children and their families can take part in the services the government offers, or to provide services in places the government is unable to reach. Going to School in India features government schools, community schools, and educational activities supported by NGOs. There are other kinds of schools in India as well, including private schools and religious schools. Limited space made it impossible to include examples of all of them in this book. The names of the NGOs that support the programs in this book are included just after the name and location of the school at the beginning of each chapter.